Okie Chronicles

Okie Chronicles

Pamela Harrison

David Robert Books

Published by David Robert Books
P.O. Box 541106
Cincinnati, OH 45254-1106

Typeset in Aldine by WordTech Communications LLC,
Cincinnati, OH

ISBN: 1932339876
LCCN: 2004098622

Poetry Editor: Kevin Walzer
Business Editor: Lori Jareo

Visit us on the web at www.davidrobertbooks.com

Cover image: © Morris Galloway 2005
Author photo: Lia Rothstein

Acknowledgments

Grateful acknowledgment is made to the editors of the following magazines in which some of these poems first appeared:

Great River Review: "The Gist of It" (as "Prissy Ziegler Catches Her Coat"); "Saturday" (as "Lucy Mae gets her head stuck"); "Sure Shot" (as "Betty's Smashing Place"); "What It Was"; "Prospects"; and "The Cowgirl Blues" (as "The Whole Shooting Match")

The Midwest Quarterly: "Alien Corn"

Passages North: "Sunday" (as "Chicken and Dumplings")

I am grateful to the MacDowell Colony, the Vermont Studio Center, and Lisa Stokes Taylor for providing space and time to begin this book. Thanks especially to Cleopatra Mathis, Carol Westberg, Barbara Dimmick, and Heather Bagley for their encouragement and invaluable critique; to my brother and sister for their abiding affection; and to the people of Oklahoma for their inspiration.

In memory of my mother and father,
Vera Alice Pritchett and Lynn Henry Harrison

Characters

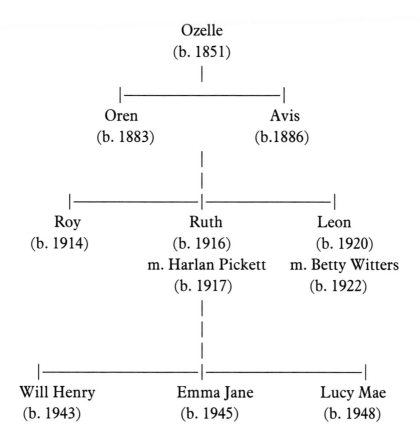

Ozelle
(b. 1851)

Oren
(b. 1883)

Avis
(b.1886)

Roy
(b. 1914)

Ruth
(b. 1916)
m. Harlan Pickett
(b. 1917)

Leon
(b. 1920)
m. Betty Witters
(b. 1922)

Will Henry
(b. 1943)

Emma Jane
(b. 1945)

Lucy Mae
(b. 1948)

Doreen McCann
(b. 1932)

Contents

Prologue
Borderland..17
Ozelle...19

I. 1952
Alien Corn 25
Her Piano 27
What Betty Saw...28
Family 29
The Way She Was 30
Ruth Says Goodbye 31
Her Mangle 33
Prospects..34
The Long Haul...35
Leon, First Grade...36
What He's Up To..38
Watermelon...39
Tonsils 41
Pinochle Night 42
The Gist of It...43
Grudging Angels..45

II. 1954

Trespass...49

Leon's Big Deal..51

Sure Shot..52

The Day the Brethren Come 53

Saturday 55

Sunday..56

Barren 58

Life, Like a Wolf......................................59

How It Starts...61

Doreen thinks men 62

Leon Makes Lunch....................................63

Better Homes and Gardens........................64

The Watchers...65

The Forecast 66

First Snow...68

Will Grows Tall 69

Her Cool Remove 70

Veal...71

Presley Pig..72

III. 1955-56

Unplucked Music......................................77

Leon thinks 78

Leon Loads Hog..79

The Cowgirl Blues 80

The Good Woman Blues 81

O...82

Monday...83

Drought..84

Blue Ribbons...86

Doreen, Dance Night 88
Betty remembers 89
What It Was 90
Blue Serenade 91
Paradise Motel 92
Blue Chenille 93
Ashes 94
Redress 95
Bedrock 96
Blue Sky 97

Prologue

Borderland

Where the rumple of the Ozarks
smooths to the prairie plain, on the border
of South and West—mockingbirds
call down the chimney at dawn.
The sun's engine rumbles up the curve,
glare and heat rush over the flats
faster than jackrabbits routed by fire.

Caught, the tops of cottonwood trees,
then the fragrant Osage orange, soon all
the long grass. A dry blast of light
blazes the way to dusk, the western rim
unfurls red banners for the just-spent day,
and the purple earth dissolves
before the long roll of night.

Between these poles stretches a windy space
on whose horizon, between soil and sky,
men and women bend, scratching shallow names
in the plain. No wonder they don't say much,
and when they do, it's for the story they ply
against the emptiness that laps on every side.

That-he-is-able a man takes with him
like a totem to the fields. At midday,
sun falls straight on his shoulders,
and he stands on the sill of his own shadow,
sufficient as it might prove.

Ozelle

1889: The Run

In the low basement of the boarding house,
she ducked the slap of dripping sleeves, earning
her weekly keep scrubbing her knuckles raw.
When the baby's moon face caught her crying
as she drubbed some cowboy's stinking clothes,
Oz determined to pawn her last good things
for a buckboard and mare to head west
to the Indian land grab with the other
dreamers, losers, misfits, and cons.

Roping her children down on a mattress,
she tightened her bonnet and lit out at noon
to April twenty-second's tune of bugles and guns.
Land-mad fools on horses and mules, wagons,
buggies, and bikes spilled out like an army of ants
over the plain, all crazed to stake their claim.
Little Oren held his hands to his ears, Avis wailed.
In the crush, braces snapped and axles cracked,
frightened animals squealed and fell.

Grit in her teeth, sod in her hair, Ozelle
steered toward the shimmer of instant cities.
She drove her stake as the sun slid down
and sat the children in the tent to hold it.

Too suspicious of any man's intentions
to believe the gent who warned her claim
was out of line, she hunkered squatting
in what became the Main Street of Chandler
till mule teams and laughter drove her away.

1928

Life's nothing but a split pail.
Why, she knew of a man whose house and kin
blew off in a storm while he knelt
in the cellar sorting spuds. Days later,

like a lone oak leaf spiraling slowly
out of nowhere to the ground,
his Sunday hat floated down
nigh where he was standing.

Most times that's all the thanks you ever get.
Like she told that daughter of hers—*Avis,
you marry that man you'll learn the meaning
of remorse, rue it to your dying day.*

The girl just swept the grit out the screen door
and never said a word till it was done
and the first baby born.
Named for his ma.

Then Oren ran off with that Parnell girl.
Easy to see what they was after.

He's rued it, too. She's got the same splayed eyes
her momma had when they found her

dressed in nothing but white gloves
and watering the horsehair sofa with a garden hose.

I. 1952

Alien Corn

Shouldered between her elders on the bench,
Betty listened to their sins and mourned,
fearing how the end might come, that Last Day
dawning while they worked the fields, her shoes

and skirt wet with morning dew, broken clouds
trailing from the east onto the shadowed land,
magpies calling, Day Star dislodged, the crack
of hell spreading as she fled down the row.

After sermon, she bathed their calloused feet—
ankles wrinkled white and hairless, toenails
yellow and thick with age, as sharp as claws—
bending so low she hid them with her hair.

"Mind what I mark, girl," Aunt Ada warned,
ruling red lines under verses to heed:
filthy dreamers defile the flesh, despise
dominion, speak evil of dignities—

and there, under a fanning mimosa,
while summer's cicadas sang lazy hymns
and pink blossoms floated down amber air,
Betty knew herself a dreamer, damned.

Ada stood behind her as she knelt to prayers,
pushing Betty's head to the quilt with her hand.
Outside, the windmill tugged hard on its chain,
rusty gears startled by a rising wind.

Her Piano

Betty couldn't remember a time she didn't play,
had known before knowing what was hers,
as though music welled like riches in her hands.

And though her gift was spent on coaxing
notes from country kids' cramped hands,
she still delighted in their first approach to song.

Marches for the boy in Buster Browns,
rain-soaked studies for the serious girl
whose inner life had found no words—

Betty sent them humming out the door, then
played for her own pleasure, notes spilling out
the open windows until evening closed

and shadows curled into the corners of the room.

What Betty Saw

Maybe it was because she had no children,
because she waited, open like the land
to conceive, because she saw Leon beyond
his half-baked plans and foolishness

as a man whose dreams might any day spring
like a geyser, refreshing everything.
He was the frontier, last run of broken dreams,
who yet embodied, beneath the dust and drudge,

the hope of change. He'd prove in the trial.
Watching his long silhouette as it moved
between the house and barn, lit from behind
by the winking sun, Betty felt something

close to honor, as though he alone bridged
the bare back of those windy plains
with the starred and endless reaches of the sky.

Family

Looking around the table
at their faces as they ate—
Willie building castles of potatoes,
Emma herding peas to keep it neat,
Lucy eating three bites each, Ruth
passing her butter biscuits, and
Leon's jaw knotted on the beef—
Betty saw all their chins alike,
all their long jaws and teeth,
brows and ear lobes of a piece.

Despite variations in their hair
and fairness, there was something
running through them, some
sameness in the blood, and
Betty never felt so strange
or lonely as she did then,
the one outsider, married in.

Close up, everyone clouded,
hard to read as far mirages.
For all they shared, she guessed,
every one of them was lonely,
disposed against a vacancy
each only hoped to fill.

The Way She Was

When Ruth was maybe twelve—
old enough to know her dream
of finding fairies under cabbage leaves
was hogwash, soon after her dog died
of snakebite, and Avis no longer
let her wear her brother's clothes—

she wouldn't answer to any name
but *Jimmy*, and took up smokes,
rolling her own behind the barn.
But it was no good. If she had to be a girl,
well then, she wouldn't be a Baptist, too.
She'd play cards, swear if need be,
and dance all night when she pleased.

Ruth Says Goodbye

When she got her husband's letter, she left
the kids with Leon and Betty and caught
the long bus to meet him in California.
Working shifts, she roomed with her brother Roy
and waited for Harlan to show, which he did,
drunk, one Friday supper, slung on the swing
like a sack of spoiled potatoes. Roy grabbed
a baseball bat and barred him at the door.

Ruth pulled Harlan shambling up the streets
until he sobered enough to talk. They sat
under the fragrant clack of a gum tree
and watched the stars come on like city lights.
Ruth told about the kids, showed photos,
especially Lucy, the child he'd never seen.
Harlan leaned with a groan against the tree.
Sweat stained his shirt, his khaki pants were soiled.

He cried to think what he had come to, through
the stinking war, fungus, leeches, maggots,
Zombie Marine left too long on Bataan.
He longed to bury his face in her skirt. This time
she didn't stroke his hair, murmuring he'd find his way
back home. She looked at the tiny pinprick stars
and thought they looked like the red sparks
that flew up when a burning house fell in.

She felt cool breezes sliding downhill, rustling
the dry leaves. This was the last trip, her last try.
But she would keep his name and wear his ring,
and his handsome, uniformed picture
would hang by her bed to the end of her days.

Her Mangle

Ruth plays it Tuesdays like Miss Helms
at Sunday hymns, fingers fluttering white
as cabbage moths between the searing steel,
long padded roller, and leap of steam.

One, two—the roller rises, she squares
the sheets, leans her knee right to the lever;
three, four—the roller lowers, pressing down.
In the quick of time, her hands lift away.

Ruth keeps the beat for hours, until sweat
slaps her on the back and damp curls wind
tight as grape vines at her temple. Heat fogs
the top of every kitchen window.

Mrs. McLeod will pay her a dollar short,
certain any woman unlucky enough
to eke by doing her betters' wash
would not perform to standards of the saved.

Prospects

He'd hauled enough cement to know
the weight of a hard-earned dollar,
driven rigs on back roads to shake the fuzz,
lived for days on fries and No-Doz.
Ranch hand, combines, oilfields, construction:

if work could make it happen, Leon would.
Raised a scrap-bag, Okie farm boy,
he vowed, when he saw a Comanche
driving a Cadillac crowned with longhorns,
he'd own a Caddy someday, too.

Wherever the boom went, he followed,
back pay burning holes in his pants till
he could buy something new to show—tooled
boots, hats, a dress for Betty, and cars
he lost on credit when the job dissolved.

He rode boom and bust like a bronc buster,
some slower out of the chute each year,
bow-legged, creaking. "Prospects," he would say.
He always had prospects, thumbs dug in his belt,
nosing the toe of his boot into the dirt

and squinting into the sunset
like no tomorrow.

The Long Haul

Betty called him to his best,
knew when he slacked off
or sold himself a bill of goods
and seldom had to say it.

Just looked at him with eyes
that bored clear through his head
or pierced his heart with shame.

She was the standard he looked to,
the one he strove to please.
The break of her occasional smile
soothed him like sun-lit rain.

What pleased her he could never tell.
Not the gifts he loved to give. She
shook her head like he hadn't got it right.

But sometimes riding in the truck,
she'd pat his thigh, spreading
warmth to all his parts, or come behind
when he stood looking off alone

and rest her head upon his back.
It was that urgency he answered.

Leon, First Grade

He jumped at the clipped commands
of the marm who beat a ruler in her palm.
His bitten yellow pencil scratched letters
she chalked smoothly on the board.

Autumn leaves fall from the trees
her sentence read, and all the treeless,
gold-grassed October morning
leaned with him to his task.

"Don't press so hard. You'll tear it."
He bent to the burden, witlessly
sucking his thumb as he scrawled
the crawling shapes of sound.

Then it wasn't tearing he heard.
More a hiss, as though the radiator
came suddenly alive beside him,
like the dangerous snakes that coiled

on the sunlit porch of his house. It was
the hiss of the teacher as she dragged him
to stand against the alphabet,
and held his culprit thumb up high.

The room filled with fiery autumn light,
as though a forest of trees ignited at a cue,
and he was tied to one of those fabled trees.
Flames rose from his socks to his knees,

from his knees to his chin,
from his chin to the roots of his hair.

What He's Up To

When she gets the call, Ruth looks around
expecting to see her kids buzzing
like gnats in her wake, but the sheriff says
Will's been leading the wagons astray
and two miles from home is two too far.

Hours after that wrong turn,
Ruth catches Will Henry
lighting matches under his bed sheet.
Thinking excess will cure him,
she makes him strike a whole box of Blue Tips.

Will thinks playing with fire's so fun,
next day he puts a match to the trash
piled beneath the pine out back.
Ruth looks up from her wash
to find a tree burning in the wilderness.

Before the brigade can douse the flames,
Ruth burns a firebreak on the boy's backside.
For days, Will's got such a singe on his pride,
he sets a spark to every short fuse he can find.
He still likes matches.

Watermelon

Summer sears.
Leon mows hay till
his socks sag and sweat drips
from the tip of his bony nose.

The dog pants on the porch floor.
Lucy Mae and Emma Jane
toe the green glider in time
to the locusts' drone.

"Let's go," Leon says,
slapping his hat on his hip,
spraying sweat on the step.
They pile in and head for Teeters'.

"That one," Leon says,
giving its side a thwack.
Green torpedoes dip and roll
with the icebergs in the tank.

The kids lean against the cool
like bugs splayed on a windscreen.
Leon plugs a beauty
and slices it up all round.

They fork the pink sweet down,
spitting seeds and shooing flies.

The day turns inside out.
Six rinds smile on the board.

Tonsils

Leon says, "Come for a ride."
Next thing Emma Jane knows,
she's strapped on her back and
wheeled through the halls while
some bandit in a white mask counts
backwards.
                Emma Jane wakes
back home with a bear trap
clamped on her throat. Mother
gives her Aspergum and ice cream.
Betty gives her Chinese pajamas.
Leon's nowhere to be seen.

Pinochle Night

Bowls of chocolate-covered nuts
stud the four corners of the table.
Cigarette smoke winds like corkscrews
to a dusky, low-flying cloud.

All the neighbor ladies' faces
freeze over their cards.
Everyone but Ruth
backs away over their chairs

when Will Henry
lays the snake
like a necklace
around her neck.

It licks at her chin.
"Take...it...away," she says,
so low and cold and slow,
he'll never again take her for granted.

The Gist of It

Leon says, "It was an awful shame."
Betty says, "It was mink

and full-length, and Prissy
had no business with it

on a camping trip." Night fell.
The old Arbuckle mountains

slept on their sides, breathing
gently in the dark. Campfire crackled,

and they all told dirty jokes
and drank bootlegged hootch

till the chill came down
and Prissy called for her coat.

Someone—some said it was Ed
himself—threw her the coat,

but the toss went wrong.
Prissy leaned to catch it, and coat

and Prissy both fell backward
off the cliff into the dark.

Leon said, "She died quick."
Betty said, "She caught the coat."

Grudging Angels

Leon couldn't say what held him to it.
It was his harness, love or hate,
and he wrestled it daily, grudging
the life he took such pains to make.

After working hours mending fence,
he'd straighten and look long west,
gathering patience through his boots
to quiet the rage in his chest,

as though strength rose from the very land
that broke his hopes when rains came late.
He loved heat-baked days, light lifting in waves
over heavy-headed wheat—

like everything on earth wore haloes—closest
they'd ever get to God, whom he feared
but couldn't trust. No. Just dust, luck,
and the stubborn pluck of his own pride.

★

Summer days the glare was so bad
it made Betty sneeze to walk into the light.
Her eyes clamped shut, screwing her face
into a squint smocked tight as the wizened
Indian who tended Prouty's stock.

The spank of it stung harder by the hour.
Nothing was saved from the sun's assault.
By the high hammer of noon, even the sparrows
were stunned to silence, the ground tanned to cowhide,
field grass bleached white as the hair on Leon's arm.

But, ah, the fall of dusk—when the wind
died down and the worry of dry leaves relaxed.
The mimosa's cool perfume wafted in waves
over the darkened yard. The earth eased,
like her own dry skin when they made love—

rough-to-touch come satin.

II. 1954

Trespass

At first she thought it one of Willie's toys,
fat sausages wound on the icebox top,
except the heavy head lifted,
the split tongue wagged,
coils slid to tighten their repose.

When the hair on her head lay down,
Betty felt the strangest sort of wonder,
eye to eye with dread in her own house:
snake and woman equally entranced
as though the thing bore meanings.

The sleepy head settled, watching
for her move. She wasn't superstitious
but had a patch of Cherokee that paid attention
when critters came indoors. Surely, it was hers.
Why else would everyone be gone?

She laughed then suddenly, out loud, so sharp
the serpent stirred, a soft rattle of its tail.
Some Eden, she thought, smiling
at the smugness of it, at the bully confidence
of the evil creature's lassitude.

Well, whatever the snake might be,
it was Betty's house.
With hatchet, hammer and mop,
Betty dispatched it quick
and flung it to the crows.

Leon's Big Deal

Sighting the red rooster tail of his dust
flying the length of the county road,
they drop their chores and gather at the drive

to welcome Leon home. Months in Mexico
wildcatting, now driving a Cadillac convertible,
turquoise blue, with fins flaunted higher

than a cow pony's tail. Black trooper sunglasses and
a thin mustache—this cool new dude leans back.
Teeth flash in a leather-brown face.

No one knows for absolute sure it's him.
He insists. Betty sits
stiff as a corn cob on the seat.

Sure Shot

Years ago she hit the barn wall so hard
she broke a bone in her fist and wore a splint
for weeks, half-trophy, half penance. Those were days
her anger surged against him monthly, buried hurts
she thought on better days to overlook.

When she seethed instead of speaking, reasons
capped and bottled in her throat, he'd coax her
to talk, taking her wrath until it cooled
and she subsided in his arms to weep.
She never knew the strength it cost him.

Older now, she's made a smashing place
in a corner of the barn where she gathers empty jars
and bottles from the house. Quietly, she disappears
down there, pitching bottles one by one against the wall.
A five-bottle fume—she enters laughing.

A twenty-bottle rage, and the words
she hurls at him are cold and like to kill.

The Day the Brethren Come

Betty is sweeping nests of spiders
from the corners of Ruth's front porch when
a crow-black sedan rolls in off the road,
two brethren up front in shirts and ties,
two sisters behind in Sabbath dresses.

Lucy looks up from her dolls. Betty moves
to the stoop, holding the broom in both hands.
Dust blows in as the strange car shivers to a stop.
When the back doors open like oily wings,
Betty can see by the Bibles what they want.

They hatch adders' eggs, weave the spider's web
echoes in her head as the sisters march up,
toes sharp on the path, stepping over cracks.
They hold their Bibles hard against their hearts.
"What do you think of the world today, Missus?"

Betty allows, "July's been more than ordinary hot,
and the wheat could use some rain before too long."
She hears summer's locusts sawing on the breeze
that riffles the tender curls at Lucy's neck.
She'd rather, now, Leon had left the dog.

"Omens have been given; signs are clear," they warn,
thumbing quick from Genesis to Revelations.
As they talk, pinched lips purse tight across their teeth.

Betty wonders how they chew, what kind of food
they bring to table. "The great day of His wrath is come!

and the peoples will be as if burned to lime."
Betty asks, "Dug your hidey-hole deep enough?"
"Yes, and stocked it full against the scorch and plague.
You want this sweet little girl of yours to suffer?"
One sister steps toward Lucy where she plays.

Betty watches black shoes cross the boards,
thin fingers reaching—a little touch, perhaps
a palm on Lucy's head.
Like Moses ending a plague, Betty lifts her broom
and slams it to the floor so hard

the sisters yelp and flee, and she sweeps after them,
clearing the boards, the steps, the dazzling walk,
sweeping until the dark car squeals, doors flapping wide,
out the drive and down the dusty road away.
Lucy watches from the porch, amazed.

Saturday

Lucy Mae gets her head stuck
between the pickets
while Mother's at the store.

Her braids hang down like beagle ears,
longer than the streaks of her tears.
She's on her knees and begging.

While Will Henry runs for help,
Emma Jane tries the bars,
but she's no Super Girl.

She bends low to scold Lucy Mae
for being so dumb, stuck like mother's melons
grown through the wire.

Sunday

Emma knew whose chicken it was.
The coop leaned beside the barn,
plain to see, thick to smell,

festooned with scarlet roses and
alarming lumps of chicken dung;
ruled by a blind bantam rooster;

worried over by chesty hens
he pecked on the neck
till their bare skin shone like bangles.

Those bloody collars were signs
of romance, testaments
of favor, power in the roost.

She'd gathered brown eggs for breakfast
and seen a dead chicken plucked—
red dress torn for pillow feathers—

but, bursting out the back door,
she did not expect to see, right then,
Grandmother's hatchet come down hard

on the stump, clean through, as though
that collar was meant for cutting
the chicken's skinny, outstretched neck.

Flapping dance around the yard,
red blood squirting on the grass—
poor, running chicken couldn't find its head.

This was for dinner.
This was for dumplings.
This was for her.

Barren

About as likely as Harlan traipsing back after the war.
Dead or dead drunk in some bar, he's wasting
his pension on some whore while Ruth
scrapes by doing the neighbors' dirty clothes.

But Ruth's got kids, and Betty won't ever
be a whole woman for lack of them.
Ruth's breasts rest heavy in her dress.
Betty's are girlish, pale as pink roses.

Leon wants to see his seed passed on, wants
some red-faced, bawling proof of his manhood,
and her body won't give. He'd sell a cow
that wouldn't calf. And they both know it.

Life, Like a Wolf

Sometimes at night she'd hear the wail
and in the ticking dark she'd start to count,
like a child measuring the miles between
the lightning's flash and coming thunder.
In seconds, the heave of heaven's weight
leaned hard against her house, windows
sucked inward, door tugging hinge and lock.

The all-night howl was on. Betty hated it,
hated the invisible tide of its restless worry,
the tireless screech and plunder, hated the slip
of her loose music from the piano to the floor,
and how its secret hordes invaded, how,
no matter that she stuffed the cracks
or daily mopped and swept, the grit's
fine grains gained against her, piling up
on the west side of the pickets, burying
the bottom step of the porch, gathering
in tiny dunes on the coverlet, and settling
while she slept like squatters in her hair.

Most of all, as she burrowed beneath the covers
and deeper into the hollow of Leon's arm,
she hated the helpless sense she had
that her house couldn't hold against the blow,
that she, a grown woman, had come to fear
the wind like a live thing on the prowl.

She could hear it breathing about her eaves.
It was hungry and wanted in.

How It Starts

Slaving from dawn to dusk,
the two of them have scraped and painted
for days, so frying hot

atop those Conoco storage tanks,
their buttocks are burned through their jeans.
You could serve their toasted balls on toothpicks.

In a twit, Leon says, "Quit
kicking dust on our new paint job."
Dan White Claw unbends and squints.

Still hours from done, Leon and Dan
run circles around the tank. Saving his scalp
from an Apache pipe wrench

gives Leon a powerful thirst.
At the bar, he craves something cool,
thinks maybe Doreen looks good as the brew.

Doreen thinks men

are braggarts, bulldozers, and dumb lunks,
or cold fish, smug uncles, stuffed shirts.
She doesn't know which is worse,

the way they get love and sex ass backwards,
like little boys waving their dicks,
thinking longest is best. Who cares?

She'd rather have kind words and hands
that know how to pleasure, some respect
when she's right and patience when she fails.

She wants someone who fights clean and loves after.
Also a hairy chest to lean her head on and
kisses all over. Then, look out, buster,

and hang tight for the ride.

Leon Makes Lunch

Take three grilled cheese,
minus the cheese.
Add Hershey bars.

Fry both sides in butter
till the white bread goes brown
and the sweets ooze through.

Makes your tongue want to
slap your brains out clapping!
"Don't wipe those messy fingers

on your shirts, kids,
and the good women won't
guess what they missed."

Better Homes and Gardens

Nobody reckons the time Emma spends
on Betty's couch, brown Brillo-stiff tufts
itching bare legs skinned at climbing trees
and digging forts behind the barn.

The ladies' magazine on Emma's knees
repeats in its narrow spine and leaves
the wing-like span of an open Bible.
From glossy photos fine living unfurls.

The pictures draw her eye, answering a need
her mother's bare-bones home won't feed.
She steals whole pages, little Edens she hoards
like forbidden sweets beneath her bed.

High light and windows, polished wood,
sensuous curves and voluptuous cloth:
enough to blaze a path.

The Watchers

Emma Jane lies in the dark
on the hood of Leon's truck
looking for falling stars.

August breathes close on the breeze.
The moon's bright too, passing
all the parked cars of light, but

it's falling stars she's after,
making wishes she's too shy to name.
Will Henry sees something

white moving in the moonlight
of the darkened yard. It takes
a while for his heart to calm.

It's Mother in her nightgown.
In the shadows—Mother,
bending to her roses all alone.

The Forecast

Ruth dusts with one hand, vacuums
with the other. Her house is clean. So clean,
the kids won't invite anyone in
for fear they'll make a mess.

They know her temper. Watch her
like a windsock for the weather of their days.
Easy to see when the dust is up. But they
would never know, nor would she say,

what blows about her heart. Sometimes
she catches herself humming "In the Mood,"
and it all floods back, their last dance
at Tinker Field the night Harlan shipped out.

He was such a looker in his blues.
Those days she'd rather dance than eat.
When the trombones paused,
he leaned her so far back in his arms

she could see yellow balloons shining
like dizzy moons in the hangar's dome.
She thought she'd explode, wanting him
and not wanting that dance to ever end.

She broke her heel and snagged her hose
running to the car where they last made love,

where he kissed the arch of her bare foot
like he was drinking French champagne.

Ruth cuts the humming short,
draws silence around her like a cloak,
settles deep into the muffle of its folds.

First Snow

No school. After breakfast Will swings the girls
in a snow saucer, round and round so fast
they fly like skipped stones. The usual tears,
and Ruth is peeved to leave her chores.
Come in the back door with those wet boots.

Admiral Perry ear flaps tied against the wind,
Axel Hapnagel ropes eight sleds behind his Studebaker.
The neighborhood looks new from a belly-down view.
Snow-shagged elms lean like mushers south.
Axel's tire chains crunch through knee-high drifts.
Emma Jane spills, and four sleds run her over.

Dusting the tracks off her back, consoling,
Will Henry walks his crying sister home,
forgets the rules and rings the bell in front.
Mother opens a crack, yells, *Round back!*
and slams the door with a slap. Stiffening, Will
escorts Emma to the designated door.

Mother lets them in and gets the full story then,
right between her eyes, coldly aimed
by a youth who ends by saying *I hate you.*
His first judgment of her—how it stings.

Will Grows Tall

High-water jeans and his shirts won't tuck—
his hands hang large as pipe wrenches
from cuffs that flail above corded wrists.
His new voice, deep as a kettle drum,
sounds from a chest grown broad and strong.

He looks so much like Harlan now—
Ruth's stunned sometimes to see him
flash his father's famous smile.

Today, Ruth speaks in a new voice, too.
Looking into brown eyes level with her own,
she lays her hand on the young man's shoulder.
Beneath the weight of her esteem, the boy's
coltishness straightens to a watchful calm.

She'll ask no more where he's been
or what he has or hasn't done.

The heavy mantle of her expectation
fits him like the man he wants to be.
Anointed, grown inward and quiet,
the wild mischief of his boyhood
will run underground and deepen.

Her Cool Remove

More and more, Ruth talks
less and less.

Her kids think she's either deaf
or talking to God—

Ruth could have clued them.
She never talks with God.

She just takes orders.

Veal

Emma rides behind to the place
where the mother cow has calved.
Rocks in the ditch, scrub brush
and wind whistling in winter grass,
then the little white-face wobbly
on its fur-curled legs. Leon knew
just where they'd be.

They herd them slowly home,
"calm and quiet," Leon says,
not to scare the little one. He says
Emma can name it, that it's hers.
"Brocky," she thinks, seeing how
it trots and walks, trots and walks,
in spurts like a wind-up toy.

All the way home, she swims in the gift
of getting something live and all her own.
In the barn the calf pulls so hard
at the bucket's nipple, it bangs her shin.
Blue milk spills on the ground. Leon laughs.
"That's some young bull you got there, Emmie.
You feed him good, next month, he'll
fetch a pretty price at the sale."

Presley Pig

In December, after grumbling
over chapped hands and frozen slops,
even so contented a carnivore as Betty—as capable
of snatching the last strip of bacon as gnawing
her porkchop to the bone—turns a trifle skeptical.

Juicy trimmings saved from supper,
a generous hand with grain, or friendly scratch
behind the creature's hairy ears—such caring
gestures accrue a kind of weight. Carving
an animal you call by name does give you pause.

Try as she might to think him merely meat,
rude, smelly, standing ankle deep in his own food,
not, even remotely, a cherished pet...still,
his rooting presence inhabits a corner of her yard.
His suspicious little eyes, extravagantly lashed,

watch her coming and going with genuine interest.
His preposterous tail, that vanity, goes as limp
as any saint or lover in an ecstasy of appetite.
The pied porker counters her husbandry
with the question: *Who's the brute?*

★

Leon is taking his time. It's a kind of dance
they're doing out in the pen, Presley shouldering
into the stringy man's thighs, wanting a scratch
at least, expecting something. Leon takes pride
in taking one shot. He's a patient man.

They've do-si-doed for what seems like days
while Leon maneuvers the rifle barrel
square against Presley's skull. Just
the right spot behind the ear, and the boar
will drop clean for cutting.

When the shot comes, Betty's playing
Rachmaninov so loud in the house
the chords could put a crease in Leon's jeans.

III. 1955-56

Unplucked Music

Strange fate, Betty thought.
Like storms gathered to let fall showers
that never reach the ground,
this living in the space of naught:
hollow of what might have been, vacancy
and denial, the nothing, the desert,
the nowhere, the want—

What kind of character is carved
by the absence of *is*?
Sometimes her life felt
like unplucked music,
a clavier dumped in prairie grass
as the practical wagon jounced west,
one wife's insupportable dream:

a great clanging of keys
as it crushed to the ground,
random, wind-blown tones thereafter.

Leon thinks

it's pride that keeps him whole.
No matter what the bank and bosses say,
no matter how low he's sunk
in some shit hole of a job. A man can do.

He's got a rod between his legs
that makes him try harder, work longer,
fight better, and carry on,
but he's got to believe he can.

Muscle, spit, and grit, a man will stand
against the wind like a crested butte,
throw his body like a deadbolt
between his woman and her fear.

Just so she doesn't bust his balls.
Betty holds them cracking in her hand.

Leon Loads Hog

In the morning he shoves Marigold
up the ramp from behind, has to
put his shoulder to her. The sow

is cool on courting. They drive
over to the blue boar's boudoir
some miles away. Jokes all round

about the bride's reluctance. He
has to push her in the pen,
put his shoulder to it again.

Aged bacon, the boar's no fool.
He smells a live one, there
in the plaid shirt. Leon

leaps for a beam. The raunchy brute
plows to a stop below, bellowing
for his ladylove—the cowboy in boots.

Leon hangs like a corn-fed ham
from the rafter, blushes to his roots
from all the ranch hands' laughter.

The Cowgirl Blues

When Doreen was eight, she wanted to be
Annie Oakley standing tall on the back
of her speeding horse and shooting
bulls' eyes from yards away. Six-guns
hugged her hips, and her boots matched

the hand-tooling of her saddle. By sixteen,
she always got her man, spent Sundays
on the sand flats west of town, shooting
the hearts out of quarters from fifty paces
with an older man's twenty-two.

When the sun went down, raising
a sky that spread like loosestrife
over the plains, he and she moved on
to other targets, scratching every
itch their trigger fingers found.

Being a good shot and getting a man
were not as hard as she first thought.
So far as she knows that guy is still
selling cars in Ponca City and
groping girls while he reads Zane Grey.

Okay. That's mean and small to say.
In fact, he was gentle and lonely.
And Doreen's no Annie Oakley.

The Good Woman Blues

Leon knows Betty's a proud woman,
and true. Beneath her slip, her skin

shines cool and smooth as milk glass.
He strokes the curve from her waist

to her hip, kisses the pale vein at her neck,
and wants to dive into her.

But these days she's grown hard
and holds herself apart.

He has to crank her up like a Model T,
play her tits like a penny whistle.

No wonder they got no kids. A man
wants more than a dry hole to put it in.

O

Come again to mock her,
blood of her heart
falling to nothing,
falling bitterly from

that black hole
that empty circle
that barren O
that will not bloom.

The seed is lost.
She has no gift to give.
Enfolding a void
she grows old,

her body a hoax
born for dying only.
This is no sap,
no flow of promise.

An open wound
leeches life from her
in monthly drams and
dries her like a stick.

Monday

Betty hangs wash
with a quilter's eye to line,
all the socks to size and paired,

undies front side to, hankies,
towels and sheets four-square
for folding later, jeans heel up

and pockets flared, his shirts
standing on their hands, her
dresses' shoulders straight.

Everything flaps in the breeze.
Betty turns the radio high,
weeps between the sheets.

Drought

He's seen it before—watched his father's farm
crack and blow away, their cropper shack
so sifted in with dust he feared as a child
they might be buried alive some night
while dry wind howled around the seepy eaves.
Leon grew up

hungry and hell-bent to make good,
fortified his dreams with spit and bravado.
Now he panted with fear, no better than that hound
hiding in a scratch-hole below the house while the children
played in the yard with dried skulls of birds.
Even the red ants

trailed indoors for some wet. Betty and Ruth,
their hair battened in tea towels against the dust,
wiped grit from their plates and emptied drowned bugs
from kitchen table-leg traps with disgust.
It might as well have been his dreams.
All the margin, all

the fat he'd scraped from the lean bones
of dawn-to-dusk jobs, all the fixed vision
of his desperation never to look like the beaten
dog of his own dad—whose sunken white chest

at rest in the upholstered chair where he died
still shivered Leon's pride.

Every green sprout withered and dried.

Blue Ribbons

So many summers they made love
beneath the tree's green umbrella, the garden's
poppies and jays; they made wishes in sunlight,
licking salty sweat of morning chores.

But spiders ride the skirts of fall.
Yesterday, Betty blundered on a web
woven overnight across her path. Waiting
at the center, legs cocked upon the silk,

its belly blazoned with a jet-black skull—
fall's sentry stopped her dead.
Now the weather turns urgent. Leon cuts
the long grass, and she rakes straw

to warm her flowers in their winter beds.
Reaching for blankets, they wrestle in the dark
beneath this new weight. Outside,
wind wails through empty boughs.

One day next month, they'll wake to snow.
Nine years they have planted his seed
in her earth. Nine years and nothing grown.
It all goes down, goes down, and she is done.

She wakes in darkness to watch him dreaming.
She'll give away the baby clothes she sewed,

empty the trunk of every smock and quilt.
Damn the ribbons, damn the empty crib.

She cannot bear not giving what he wants.
He'll rise to light the stoves alone.

Doreen, Dance Night

Tonight on the street, the dame
who sells costume jewels and pawn,
the one in the tobacco shop who talks
like a magpie most of the time,
flags Doreen down to ask
when she'll be coming back to claim
those rhinestone studs she hocked.

A man she never liked once said
Doreen would never know who she was
until she was alone and begging someone
to make it hurt less bad. Now Leon's friend
wants her to jack him off in the hall while
others dance away their longing
in the gloom next door.

She doesn't know who she does it for.
She sees Leon whispering in Betty's ear
everything she wants to hear.
Light burns over their faces, paper moons.
Bodies turn and turn
in the music's tight corral.

Betty remembers

the night she fell for him, so deeply
drugged with love, they danced
like they were standing still. In the Cattle Chute,
smoky road house, all the young bucks
crowded close, spilling beer.

She danced with the one she loved, but
all the ranch boys smelled was *hot*. Even after
the music stopped, they kept coming on,
edgy and excited. One brushed her chair,
his crotch at her back, like she might rub off.

Leon growled like a bear and shoved him,
glared until the pack of young men broke,
cackles and hoots stitching the sweaty air.
You could smell sex everywhere.

What It Was

Once it rose like a boil to the surface,
it was only a matter of time.
It was an itch
that had to be scratched.

It wasn't love: he craved
the smell of her, her hips'
easy swing in her skirt, full lips
pouting and the breasts.

Doreen thought he was sweet,
no narrowed eyes or smirks,
no swagger when he touched her.
Yes, it was lust, pure and simple,

and they both thirsted
for a long drink at the trough.

Blue Serenade

Doreen picks iris and rambling rose,
then waits behind the dark bar until he comes,
two hours before sun-up, as they planned.

Leon drives the Caddy through the quiet.
This hour the moon's asleep and bullfrogs doze,
only the nightjars sound their soft alarms.
No one sees them lying in the long grass.

Leon smells her flowers, one by one, then
moves on to her neck and breasts, kisses them,
kisses everywhere. When Doreen wakes,
dawn's waving a gaudy painted fan.

Shaking the hayseed from his hair, Leon
sees the pond where last night's stars had shone
turn blank beside the trampled blue and gold.

Paradise Motel

So lost in the foothills
of Doreen's breasts,
Leon doesn't see,

until the door swings fully open,
the Mexican maid
staring there, mop in hand.

In the mothy yellow light,
her hair glows
in a smoky halo about her head.

The sight pulls him up so short,
he thinks he might be found there,
dead and undressed in a slattern bed.

Cursing them for not locking the door,
the maid drops a rag as she hustles away.
Leon holds it like a fig leaf to his shame.

Blue Chenille

He finds Betty standing by the window
at the far end of their house, the blue robe
he bought her folded close, an envelope
sealed on the secret letter of his shame.

By starlight, the curves of her shoulder and hip
are hard as marble, blue as the smoke
curling in the stillness from her cigarette.

She stares into the dark, wrapped in a hurt
so speechless and deep he longs
for any vessel of feeling to rise
from the lightless mine of her heart.

He has done this to them, willfully, carelessly,
and now stands waiting to be recognized, waiting
for the stony absence of any word to crack.

Ashes

Betty shuts the piano
and turns away.

No solace in it.
She cannot play

an instrument gone
dead beneath her hand.

The empty notes grate
like wind-driven sand.

She trails the light
from window to window—

looking for what? A song
whose cadenced glow

fades by the hour,
a rhythm in the bass

that bound one moment
to the next—erased.

Redress

Betty rocks back and forth
over cracks in the floor.
Rupture rises in her gullet.

She wants to smash something,
throw buckets of paint
in black X's on their bed.

Hurt pride craves redress,
and she must soon
decide how much.

She knows she's the only
woman for Leon, the girl
was never an earnest rival.

In time, she takes her shears
to Leon's jeans.
Slung on the couch

when he comes home,
all his crotches are air-conditioned.
Betty's some improved.

Bedrock

In the slanted cast of evening light
beneath the swoop and flight of scissortails,

Leon watches the stormy courses of the sky
disperse above the patient land.

Pushing past the rusted screen,
he joins Betty after supper on the porch

grateful that she will stay—
that they still share a husbandry

that uses every last thing up
before throwing it away.

Blue Sky

When the low rooms pinched
and she thought she'd suffocate
in the linty rub of family ties,

Betty dropped them like a lead bucket
and strode out the back door
to the far rise of the field. There,

in the lonely sough of dry grass,
beneath the expanse of blue sky
that vexed Leon and chafed his pride,

all the wadded, knotted tangle
of their humanness shrank to nothing.
Seeing her refuge

bathed in that vastness and light,
she knew how small she was
in God's own eye: sky, space,

the emergent urge from which her life
miraculously sprang and to which
it would be gathered back.

Like coming home after bitter journeys,
sleeping in her own bed and clean sheets.

Born and raised in Oklahoma, Pamela Harrison is the granddaughter of settlers who participated in the 1889 Land Run. A graduate of Smith College and the Vermont College MFA Program in Writing, she won the PEN New England North Discovery Poet Award in 2002. Her first book, *Stereopticon*, was published by David Robert Books in 2004. Ms. Harrison lives with her husband in Norwich, Vermont.

CPSIA information can be obtained at www.ICGtesting.com
Printed in the USA
LVOW040941020112

261887LV00001B/26/A